Table of Contents

Foreword

The author, William Vannordstrand, worked several years as a Purchasing Agent for a large high volume manufacturer of power equipment before going to work in sales for a nationally known and ranked manufacturer of die-cut parts. His new company serviced most of the eastern United States, expanding into the Midwest. Travel included all the way from the east coast to the central United States and just about anywhere that held good prospects.

Thirty years of selling to a wide variety of OEM manufacturers has produced a deep knowledge base and realm of reference due to the many experiences he has encountered in the field.

The author's continuous dedication and reinvention of company sales practices more than doubled the entire company's monetary sales volume, necessitated building another facility in

the south, and eclipsed all other salesmen in the company's

history to this day.

Introduction

I wrote this book mainly because I was urged to. I received my beginning business education while I was employed in the purchasing department of a large manufacturing company. I had complete responsibility for purchasing many millions of dollars of various commodities and witnessed over the years many mistakes made by salespeople calling on me. I never forgot them and, when I went into sales, I tried to avoid these blunders. When I did change over to the other side, I had a pretty successful career in selling for about 30 years, and some people think that I should pass some of my insights on to others. I think that lots of what I have to say is accepted by good salespeople and that they will recognize the truths in what I say and maybe even think," I know that." I thought the same way in most seminars I ever attended or with tapes I listened to about selling. Many times I found errors and untruths in the presentations. The bottom line though is that everyone cannot sell like everyone else. Individual salespeople need to develop their own techniques, but this is much easier to do if you listen to other salespeople's stories of mistakes as well as their successes.

In this book I will make reference to most people in the male gender. It gets tedious constantly inserting (or her) every time I make a reference to a nameless individual. I know that most readers don't really care so that's what I have done.

Chapter One:

Don't Take It the Wrong Way

How many times have you heard a prospective customer say, **"I'm sorry, we already have a good supplier that we are very happy with."** I hate to think of how many salesmen are turned off by that phrase. This is the EXACT line that you want your customers saying to YOUR competitors! This guy is the perfect customer, and you have accomplished the first step. You found him. Do you know what I do? I tell this guy that he is my type of customer. He is a person who is loyal to a good supplier, and not one to just jump up and buy from the first low balling price guy that happens along. I say that I intend to earn his respect, and that if ever he wants to try *another* good supplier, I am there for him. If he will have lunch with me the next time I come by, I would like to tell him more about my company, and if sometime in the future he ever needs a second or backup source...well. I **promise** you this. If this soon to be prospect has lunch with me, he has already taken the first step in my direction, and I am just about 100 percent certain that I will do business here. Don't screw up at lunch. If you don't know how to handle that first business lunch, you probably don't need to read any further. Remember, very few buyers will go to lunch with you without considering you as a supplier. I know that every now and then there is some guy who just wants a free meal, but if he is a really good prospect, the playing ground is level. You just might be the one getting the free lunch.

The other side of this example is the "potential" customer who has lots of good business, and when you walk through the door, he gives you a big package of prints to quote. This happened to me once with a huge lighting manufacturer; there were about a hundred prints in the package and, of course, every one of them had been handed out numerous times. The buyer was already purchasing them all at a cost that left marginal profit to anyone except the guy who had *all* the business. I was young and very proud of the package that I brought in (that would take weeks to estimate prices and quote). The owner of my company had already" been there and done that" as the saying goes. He told me that we were not going to quote because even if we were fortunate enough to be the low bidder, and get a couple of the parts, we would only have the business until the next guy came along and made a mistake and quoted the package. I was disappointed at the time but with time and experience, I learned that my boss was correct. We did not need a customer that thinks loyalty is Queen Elizabeth's family.

Lesson learned: If *a potential customer hands out blueprints or RFQs like invitations to a Senior Citizen Finance Luncheon, beware.*

Chapter 2:

The Three Big Things

This is supposed to be a book about selling, at least my version of what it takes and how I was successful. In my opinion, the **one** big requirement to be successful is to work for a good company or represent a good product. If you sell tons of stuff and your company lets you down, then what was gained? Your reputation is damaged with all of the now ex-customers. An example being making a huge sale to Wal-Mart of some new soft drink and then finding out the stuff not only tastes terrible but was shipped late and mis-billed. Goodbye Wal-Mart. Plus, the buyer now hates you because you have also made him (or her) look bad. You *need* to work for an ethical and reliable company or sooner or later it will come back to bite you.

Wait a minute; actually there are **two** big requirements. You have to be able to sell and sort of enjoy it. Some people are square pegs in round holes, and they are trying to sell even though they are not truly cut out for it. It will eventually surface and then you will have to try and find a job in a field you are suitable for. It's too bad if you wasted a lot of time.

I once had to make a sales call with this factory sales guy from a company we represented. Since I was friends with the customer, I asked this guy if he minded if I did the initial talking, and he could answer any questions. We were half way to the customer at the time. This guy turned crimson and got a look on his face like Jack Nicholson in The Shining. He screamed at me not to tell him what to do! Geez! I was caught off guard. I had several unpleasant thoughts about what I wanted to do this guy but somehow managed to turn around and drive this maniac back to his car. I was not taking him anywhere near my customer. I just knew nobody at my company would believe what had happened. I fully expected to be asked what terrible thing I had done to cause this to happen. Even *I* would not have believed me. The point of all of this is that this guy was not cut out for sales.

Epilogue: Soon after this incident the guy was either fired or quit and went into business for himself. He must not have been able to work with himself either because that same year he beat me to the punch and shot himself. Some people that act crazy, really are. Sometimes they are salespeople. Of course this story is an extreme, but it makes the point about being cut out for selling. Oops, now that I think about it, there is actually another important factor in selling and now that I think about it, **it** is the number **one** thing: **People must like you**. If people do not like you, then even if you work for this great company and you enjoy selling, then you only have the business until the second that someone they like comes along that can supply the same or similar product. Yes, for sure that is the **number one thing,** no matter what.

Summing this all up the prerequisites are pretty simple:

1. People must like you.

2. You must work for a decent company.

3. You must have a predilection for sales which dictates that you socialize with your customers.

Chapter Three:

Being Prepared

I have read many books, been to seminars, and listened to how-to sell recordings. I agree with most of what is said, but I never really listened to learn. I listened to see if I agreed or not. I always thought I knew as much or more than the speaker or author, and when I disagreed with them, I'd mull it over and see if I thought I could be wrong. I would often run the issue by my boss. He sometimes went with me on sales calls but never actually claimed to be a salesman. He was more of a listener and problem solver. It is interesting to note that when we read the same book or attended the same seminar, he got something different out of it than I did. One of the best things about him was that when we disagreed on something, he would always listen to what I thought the issue was and think it over and was never afraid to tell me that after consideration if he thought I was right. You don't run into many people like that. Anyway, talking it over with him often solidified my belief, and I think made me a better salesman.

When you can develop a relationship with someone who has different views on things, it can be a big help in negotiating. You can often iron out problems that may come up prior to the negotiations. At least you can anticipate them and have some sort of approach to a solution. For instance, my boss used to think that the customer was going to go along with a proposal because it made sense to him. I, on the other hand, knew the customer much better and felt that no matter how much sense it made, the customer would probably react in a different way. When we talked these views over, often we would have a plan in mind no matter which way the negotiations went. Nevertheless, we were *always* amazed at our prowess when things went just as we expected…good or bad.

Bottom line: Have a plan. Any plan is better than no plan, but try not to have a bad plan.

Chapter Four:

Can You Get A New Account?

The other day I had lunch with my ex-boss, and he asked me how I was able to call on a potential customer only **one** time and more often than not tell immediately that I would be able to get good business from the account or not. The short answer is "learned instinct." I got along well in the introduction, so it tends to support that I can get some business. That is not necessarily always the case, especially if the competitor is well liked. My *real* answer to this is that I usually actually ask the buyers, "Can I do some business with you?" If he says "Yes," then there is no problem, and if he says "No," then there is a problem, but since I know about it, maybe I can solve it.

One of my selling concepts is one I call "Making the Customer Say No." If you ask about your price, your service, anything, and the customer says," No" (or something negative), then you have the opportunity to solve whatever is wrong. If you (Chapter 1) work for a good reliable company and the customer likes you, then finding out what the obstacle is should not be a problem. It never was for me.

Let's say the problem is that you have been asked to quote, and your price is high. The buyer has told you already that he *does not* give pricing information out on quotations. Let's say that you ask in response, "Does that mean if I get my price in line, I can get this order?" The buyer's response is "No." Ouch! That sounds like a door closing, but I always looked at it like a door opening. At least **now** you know it is something other than not being the low bidder.

I know that the real problem may be that the guy is buying from his brother-in law, and he will not reveal this because it makes him look bad, so he will fabricate some other notion. Yes, you may never find this out, but this is an exception to the rule. What salesmen need to operate on is what is going on ***most*** of the time, not exceptions. Most of the time it is a reason like someone else has already supplied free samples. Now the customer feels obligated to place the order with the guy. I actually agree with this premise, but not so much that I will not try and get the business anyway.

Let's review: the buyer likes you enough to let you quote, and he likes you enough to tell you the reason that the competitor is getting this order, so you have all the information you need to get an order for the next item up for bid. (You can try and get the second order on this current part but that will mostly just come naturally after you start doing business with this company). My next question to the buyer is about which other parts the company will need samples on and when can **I** send them. Remember: *No buyer in his right mind will give you all of this information unless he intends to give you a shot at the business. Why should he?*

Back to the top, if you want business, ask for it. If you get a negative, ask why. If I were your boss, I would surely ask you why. If you disagree with anything above, maybe you should think about it more.

Paradox

Making a customer say "No" is a good technique but a customer saying "No" is bad. The lesson here is to differentiate and understand that when a customer says "No" to your bid, he will seldom change his mind and say "Yes" because you have persuaded him to. He may do it if it is *his* decision. For instance, if his first choice supplier has let him down in some way and he *has* to make a new choice, then you might be the one.

If the order is huge and your only option is begging to get another chance, you might have to go that way. If you have other options, take them. I just think that the buyer will feel that if he changes his mind under pressure from a seller, he has been manipulated into doing so, and that will never be a good thing. In 30 years I seldom saw a buyer change his "No" to "Yes" unless he thought it was entirely his own idea. They **always** had a good reason.

I can remember a time when I was somehow the low bidder, and my competitor was told that they were not getting the business. The competitor's price went down faster than a Times Square hooker, but the buyer never even blinked. He had already made his decision, and it was in concrete. I was a believer, and I still am.

Lesson Learned: Recognize the opportunity that a "No" response gives you.

Chapter Five:

Escape from Eggo Foods

I was in my mid-twenties and no *real* professional salesman, but I did have a pretty good knowledge of the products my company sold. One was the well-known Lubriplate lubricants. You may not recognize the name, but it is the white stuff on most car doors, and a tube was in the butt plate of most all WWII rifles. It is used in many food manufacturing plants because it is non-toxic. If it gets in the food, it won't kill you. You can eat it on a cracker as long as you are within 50 feet of a bathroom.

Anyway, I was called out to the Eggo Foods waffle manufacturing plant to solve a question of mis-packaged gear oil. They said that the oil they just received from us was not the same color as previous oil shipments. They NEVER let you go back to the production area in this Eggo plant because of the strict cleanliness rules…unless it is absolutely necessary. Well, the guy in charge of maintenance was not there, and his bantam young assistant came to the lobby to tell me about the problem. I told him that I would have to see the oil to make any kind of judgment. He finally reluctantly agreed to let me come back "for a minute." I didn't have a hat, so they made me wear one of those baker hats that look like a big white mushroom. I was glad nobody knew me.

When we got to the maintenance room, it was as white and clean as a hospital operating room. The sink and workbenches were sparkling stainless steel and spotless. Tiny Tim showed me two glass containers of oil from the two batches. I must interrupt this story here to explain why I have mentioned this guy's size twice now, and it's like it doesn't have anything to do with the story. Well, it kind of does. I am not that big of a guy either and as things progress from bad to worse, and if a fight breaks out, I think that I can take this guy as long as it is not a fair fight. Fortunately, it does not come to that. Now back to the story: One sample of the oil was in a much bigger container. I told this guy that you could not compare color of any two liquids unless they are in the same size glass containers. I was really proud of myself for this evaluation because I realized that it might even be true. I asked for the container that the new oil had come in, and it was a five gallon container. It had a pour spout so it would be a simple matter to pour a new batch in a glass beaker the same size as the old oil was in. I asked Tom Thumb for the container and told him I was going to pour another glass full, and he turned white. "Not in here!" I said I would be careful, and I was. I put the pail on the pristine counter and carefully leaned it over to dribble a glassful into the beaker. BLOOP! Jesus! Two and a half beakersful came cascading out of the spout all over the beaker, my hand, the counter and the floor. Mickey Rooney was trembling. "Oh God, Oh God! This is a clean room!"

I was worried that the oil would get on my shoes, so I was trying to set the beaker down on the counter when he grabbed it. I got a handful of paper towels and was cleaning the oil off my hand while he was swabbing up the floor. He then ran for a mop and was pouring some compound down to help absorb the spill. I kept apologizing, and he kept mumbling for us to hurry before somebody came and saw what had happened. Well, nobody came. We got the mess cleaned up like it had never happened. At least it was to the naked eye. I then asked for the beaker so I could see if it matched the other beaker and in his haste to clean up, the guy had emptied the beaker in the sink. I couldn't believe it. Now I had to pour all over again. He begged me to be careful, but since I already knew the hazard of pouring from the big pail, I was careful to just baaaarly tip it over. BLOOP! Jesus! I had done it again! Almost as bad as the first time, and when I looked at the angry face of this guy, he seemed to be somewhat taller. He spoke through gritted teeth, but still his fear of discovery was greater than his dislike for me, and he *hated* me. I had long over stayed my minute in the maintenance area when we finally got it cleaned back up the second time. This time he had the beaker upright in the sink, and I quickly got the two of them together and low and behold they were the same color. Problem solved. I was never ever allowed past the lobby area again. The good part was he didn't dare tell anyone else, so my spotless reputation was still intact with the guy who did the purchasing. This was my all-time worst sales call.

Lesson Learned: Being right is a big help in a bad situation. Try and know your stuff.

Chapter Six:

Handling a Problem Before It Happens

If you have any experience at all, you already know that if you bid, at times you will be the high bidder. I have never seen a buyer happy that he was buying from the most expensive source. They may *say* that they need the quality, so they are buying this certain item from the highest priced source on the planet. Trust me, they don't *like* it. They sometimes feel violated and often make it their life's work to find another source. It's like Osama Bin Ladin could get the business if he was the heaven sent low bidder. If you are anyone else other than the highest priced source on the planet, then you will find that you will have problems unless you can justify your pricing. This is seldom an easy thing to do if you do it *after* the bid or after the order has been awarded elsewhere. **(See Chapter Seven)**.

One solution:

I used a technique I call *Handling the Problem before It Happens*. It is simply addressing concerns that are likely to come up in the future *before* they come up. I had this good customer that was always beating me down to be the lowest bidder even though he liked the way we were always on time and saved him when he (often) ran out of parts due to sloppy planning. I came dragging into his office one day and told him I was having an awful day. He wanted to know all about it, so I let him drag it out of me that I had this good customer that was always beating me up on price even though he was a low margin account because of all the special things we had to do to get him out of trouble. I said that some people just don't seem to see the big picture and focus only on price. He was sympathetic and never once thought I was talking about him. To my knowledge, after that day, he never again hammered me on price. I realized that this was a great sales aid and used it time and time again in similar fashion. Funny thing, nobody ever made the slightest sign that they thought that they were even similar to the person in the story.

The next time that you get hammered on price, and you are not *even* the high bidder, and you did not attend to the objection long before it happened, it is your fault if you lose the order. One other thing, practice this first and don't do it if you are not good at it.

Chapter Seven:

Jackson Ready Mix

I was in my mid-twenties and discovered that everybody loves a demonstration. Even if they have no business being there, they love it because it gets them out of doing their regular work. As luck would have it, I was the guy at my company who got to learn how to operate the Luber-finer oil filter demonstration apparatus. It was really neat. It would pump nasty used oil through a Luber-finer filter, and the oil would clean up and turn back to golden before your eyes. It only took a few minutes to heat up and start the process. The worse looking the oil the better the results seemed.

I was at a large concrete ready mix facility in Atlanta and already had a demonstration set up with the shop foreman. The foreman and the mechanics were all gathered around to watch. I had participated in the demonstration several times with the factory man, but this would be my first solo performance. Just as I asked for a sample of some really bad oil from one of their trucks, some guy from the office came out and saw the crowd and yelled for the girls in the office to come out and join the festivities. I was busy pouring the dirty oil in the reservoir to be heated and pumped while the mechanics were all begrudgingly jostled aside so the interloping women could get right up front.

As God is my witness, I did not know this thing would blowback. I guess it had an air bubble in the line, so just when it was starting to pump the dirty oil the bubble blew back to the reservoir, and the result was a fine mist of the dirtiest sludge in eight states spraying every single person in the front row and several in the back. Of course the mechanics would not have cared, but it was a different story with the women. They were all running around yelling, "My skirt! My shirt! My shoes!" Jesus, you would have thought I had vomited on them. I tried not to make eye contact and kept on running the volcano. Women were scattering and mechanics were torn between the demonstration and the furor. It was like a Texas cattle stampede only in all directions and with spattered oil on the cows. In the midst of it all, the shop foreman even asked me a question. He wanted to know if it did that *every* time. He thought it was great.

I got a big sale, and every single time I made a sales call there, they would all relive the experience. I never went near the office. It was like a sales call that went bad and then got good again.

Lesson learned: If you can't please all the people, please the ones that count.

Chapter Eight:

Getting Back Lost Business

Getting back lost business. Yeah, like that's going to happen. In truth, it can happen but not often and not likely. It doesn't make much difference what the reason is or was for losing some business or, worse, an entire account. What does matter is understanding that it is mostly lost, gone forever. You will be more likely to see Mel Gibson at a Bar Mitzvah than to see lost business come back.

Why? It depends. If the business was lost because it is a regularly bid item and every year the company goes out on bid and gives it to the low bidder, yes, you could get that business back if you found a way to make the parts cheaper. What I am referring to is doing something as simple as a small price increase to see if it will fly and, the next thing you know, there are no more orders coming in on that item. In my experience, no amount of excuses and reversing the price increase will get that business back. It's lost. What is worse is that now a competitor has his foot in the door. They better wish that the competitor is not me. Whenever a buyer will make a decision to take business away like that, it is serious trouble for the current supplier. I can only say good luck in getting back to where you were.

The bottom line is to make damn sure that you *need* to do what you want to do and then try and get a feel for what the reaction will be from the customer. With a good relationship, the buyer will usually tell you right up front what the consequences will be to your action. Of course, you need to use finesse. Don't just ask if you can do it; ask in a way that gives you options and doesn't put you in a corner or on the chopping block. If the buyer likes you, you will get an answer you can count on. If not, he might ask a competitor to respond to your new game plan.

Make no mistake, getting back business that you once enjoyed and somehow lost is no easy task. It takes an unusual circumstance to get a buyer to even think about reconsidering giving you back the business once he has taken it away. You better pray that the new supplier falls down on the job.

People, especially buyers, don't like to go back and reverse a decision once it has been made but **worse** when it is their current supplier who was probably given an opportunity to keep the business and failed in that opportunity, then it is almost impossible.

I remember a time when my company experienced a slight price increase and wanted to pass it on to the customer. I was pretty tight with the customer, so I told the Purchasing Agent what we wanted to do. I was told flat out, "If we raise the price, we will lose the $250,000 worth of business." I was told this several times in the course of the conversation. I returned to my company and related the bad news. My boss asked me if I thought the customer was bluffing. I said no. I thought that since she had told me that we would lose the business, she would have little choice but to follow through. Thinking that we were secure because of our legendary past performance we raised the price anyway and lost the business. I have grieved about it for 20 years.

Now the bad part: As soon as we realized that we had lost the business, I was asked to go see what I could do about getting it back. We would *now* hold our price. I gave it a try but knew in the first minute that we would not get that business back unless something awful happened to the new supplier. Ironically, if I had been the buyer, I would have done the same thing.

Bottom line: It's better to find out why the other guy can under bid you and do something about it before you get in an ultimatum situation that is almost certain to fail.

Chapter Nine:

How I got Our Number Two Account

One of my biggest accounts of all time utilized a method I am reluctant to admit was mostly good guessing. Maybe you could say intelligent guessing since I did have a clue. First though, the buyer had to like me a little for me to be able to persuade him to do what was necessary. Let me start at the beginning.

This very lucrative and large company had lots of business spread around and was fairly satisfied the way things were. After a couple of calls on the buyer, he had given me a couple of small items to quote and was on the edge of giving me an actual order. One of the items we had quoted was a part that we had some difficulty quoting because it had a specification for a material that had to perform at some temperature that would kill an arctic seal. We finally found the material and quoted with a pretty low margin because we were trying to get started here, and that seemed like the thing to do.

I came in to follow up on our quote and was going out to lunch with the buyer. Before we could leave, he told me our price was *way* out of line high. I knew this was highly improbable given his tight material specification. I told the buyer about the material call out, and he looked at the print and saw that it said NO SUBSTITUTE MATERIAL. I told the buyer that he was most likely getting some other material, and was that allowed? He said, "Let me check." He picked up the phone and called the present supplier to ask if they made that part to print, and they said yes they did. Case closed. Well, not really. This is where my intelligent guess came into play. I told the buyer that if it was me, I would have handled that call differently. He was a good guy and asked me how I would have handled it. I said that it was not my place to accuse someone else of substituting material, but I would have bet money they were because *we* know our stuff and that material *cannot* be supplied at the pricing I am led to believe they are selling it at. I said that the other supplier just gave him a short answer and if it were me, I would call and say I needed written confirmation that they were supplying the correct material, and I needed it faxed over today. He said OK, and did just that, maybe even better than I could have done it. We then left for lunch.

Another important phase of this came during lunch when I asked him what he would do if they call back and say, "Oops we have made a small mistake and somehow we are supplying a material that is just as good but not really *specifically* like the print says." What if they say, "Tell you what, just send that stuff back, and we will replace it with the real stuff." I said they surely won't say either of those things will they? Yup.

When we returned from lunch, his assistant told him that he had several calls from the supplier requesting that he call back as soon as he could. I listened to his part of the call and lo and behold, I was right on all counts, even their excuses. The buyer got a little angry, and I got an order for the part right then.

Then I asked if it were going to cause him a problem that his cost standards were wrong because of the previous price and he will have to take a hit on that. They hate it when that happens. This account turned out to be in the top four accounts of all time at our company.

Lesson learned: If you know up front that you have a good price, use it to your advantage.

Chapter Ten:

Getting Price Feeds

I always hated it if some buyer gave my price away to a competitor, but it happens. A lot less often if you do a good job and the buyer likes you. On the other hand, I loved it when a buyer gave me pricing information. In my particular industry, there were so many ways to produce an item that knowing the price level reduced tool selection and tool size options.

It is always a big deal to know at least the price neighborhood when you go after new business. Some buyers think that revealing a competitor's price is a sacrilege. They don't consider that most all government bidding concludes with the sharing of everyone's bids so that when they announce there will be re-bidding because of some error, they all know everyone else's bid. They also don't consider that their own salesmen even go out and buy the competitor's product so they not only have a price but an actual product to copy.

I always thought the best way to get pricing information was to ask for it. I was amazed how often I was told the price right to the penny. Some buyers feel that there is no need to screw around with several bids. "Here is what I am paying, if you are so good, can you sell it cheaper?" I like that.

I can remember one time when I took my boss with me on a sales call that was happening during a time when prices kept going up, and we were caught in the middle between suppliers and customers. This particular customer had special needs such as no substitute material and packaging and stocking agreements, so it was not all cut and dried as to price. Well, they hired a new buyer who like some needed to have a showdown and went out and got bids on all of the items we were supplying. The bids were not really competitive because they did not include the packaging and stocking but were held up to us as realistic. We were told our pricing was out of line. The ironic thing is that the prices were in line with the old buyer and the one before him.

The only thing different in the equation was the new buyer, and he was mean. It was like the Spanish Inquisition only without the fancy hats.

Things started out bad and got worse. The buyer had a policy of *never* giving out price information, so when I asked how high he thought our pricing was, he said he didn't "think" anything; he knew. My boss knew already what our cost structure was on these items, and he knew our price had to be very competitive and that if we were even say, 15% high, that it was probably not apples to apples. I will cut to the chase here and say I finally got the buyer to reference **one** of the many items and tell us percentage-wise how out of line we were. Well, we were like 35% high. We knew the other bid was wrong in some way, probably substitute material, but who knows for sure? Then I told the buyer my sale-saver: (It is worth practicing and repeating ...often)

"If a buyer ever gives anyone the opportunity to get their price in line by giving them the price or something close to the price and after they see that price, they tell you: *Thanks*

but there is no way we can manufacture (or sell) the item or service for that price, <u>then they surely cannot,</u> and the price given them is probably faulty in some way." Almost *any* supplier will make every effort to match a price if given the opportunity. I know that there are some few instances that someone has some competitive edge that may knock off some of the impact of the statement above but, most of the time, it is true and buyers can grasp it, especially if they know you.

Back to the story, we *added* to the above statement that his item cost more than the price he gave us when it was still in the raw material stage. He took this seriously, and before we left, he gave us, to save face, the <u>exact percentage-high</u> price of every item on the bid.

Epilogue: He found we were correct and the bidding went away, and we gained his respect. I take credit for this great save every chance I get.

My Theory: Low bidders often have only one thing going for them, and in the long run it is usually not enough.

Chapter Eleven:

The Mole

This brings to mind the time when my office was paid a visit by a saleswoman from one of our suppliers. We had been notified in advance, and all of our management team and sales force was gathered in the conference room. This was to be a presentation to showcase this supplier's new products and to answer any questions we might have. Of course, the supplier's goal was to increase sales.

This thirtyish woman had a big black mole just above her upper lip that was immediately noticeable. In fact, it could have been noticeable from down the block. I have seen owl eyes smaller than this mole. Having been around a while you would have thought that the professionalism in the group here assembled could have ignored this mole and listened to the presentation. I know I could not. I tried to listen to her, but the mole kept getting bigger. I swear it moved when she talked. I was mesmerized. I looked around and found the entire audience was attentive and listening to the woman. I alone was transfixed on the monster mole. I did not hear a word she said. It was like someone had glued a huge grape to her face. Quasimodo would not kiss or even hug this woman.

When she finally finished up and left, all the others in the room said," What *was* that on her face?" Several tried to guess. It turns out nobody heard a word she said and to this day only refer to her as "the Mole."

Some might think that the above event is insensitive, and maybe it is. The fact is though that it really affected the presentation. This company, probably sympathetic to the woman's appearance, thought it was OK just to send her out anyway. Sympathetic, sensitive, whatever, it was poor business. There were two guys in that room who are as sympathetic as guys can get, and they couldn't recall what the woman had to say either. I thought this story was worth mentioning because I think that a scruffy pair of unpolished shoes will cause the same results.

A similar illustration of how some people having excellent knowledge of the product and market are just not cut out for sales, I will now describe in what I call the visit of The Beak.

Our sales staff was assembled in the conference room to meet a new representative from a company that we purchased raw materials from. This new guy was "promoted" from the Engineering Department of this company, and sent out on his maiden voyage so to speak, to introduce new products and services of his company. This fellow evidently had been dragging a heavy anchor for most of his life in that he had a nose on him that a Toucan would envy. He had no mustache as I am certain that nothing could grow in all that shade. Anyway, it is my opinion that he was well aware of people staring at his prominent proboscis in the past, and he expected it. He had evidently developed an attitude that caused him to react to almost everything as an attack on him because of his nose. I myself hardly noticed it except for a casual wondering if I should duck if he turned my way.

This guy actually may have been successful as a salesman, but his appearance and attitude short circuited any chance he may have had. As it turns out, several others in the room also had similar opinions and observations. We were informed of his demise in the sales field shortly after his visit. If only he could have met the Mole.

I think that this all goes along with being suited or equipped for the occupation. Why spend time in a career that has a real negative holding you back? Either fix it or go on to something else that works. You seldom see a man behind the perfume counter at a department store. You don't find illiterate people selling books. You hopefully don't find the obese marketing sporting goods. You get the picture.

Lesson learned: If you are going to hire a person to sell for you, then you should recognize anything that will hinder the goal and either hire someone else or try and fix the problem before you waste a lot of time and money.

Chapter Twelve:

Making Sales Calls with the Expert

I have had to make many sales calls with factory salespeople who most of the time had a wealth of inside knowledge about their products. Some are good and some are not so good at giving presentations. Most of them seem preoccupied with trying to write down the names and addresses of your customers.

One of the things that lots of these knowledgeable people do is belittle themselves with a statement like, "I'm no expert, but I know someone who is." That is poor judgment. Most of the times when you bring a factory guy to put on a presentation, you have a group of engineers and often executives taking their time to listen to the presentation, and they *want* to listen to an expert.

If you are taking a factory guy to put on a presentation, *tell him* that you will introduce him as an expert and *tell him* to just say thanks. Don't deny being an expert when that is what the audience wants. Don't deny it even if you are *not* an expert.

Chances are nobody will notice.

Chapter Thirteen:

A Reflection on You

Giving a gift or incentive is a good tool especially if your competitor does not. It is almost unforgivable if your competitor does and you don't.

This particular revelation may or may not be one you agree with, but if you don't think it is the gospel, then you had best think again. Never give a customer a cheap gift. Not even if it is a ballpoint pen. The quality of your gift is a direct reflection of you in the mind of the receiver. I did a study once and found that almost every single person I asked: "If a supplier gave you a nice looking pen and when you tried to use it, it wouldn't work what would go through your mind?" "That the pen was cheap and worthless," was the common answer. If you believe that it ends there, it does not. This will definitely fall back on pen giver. It is better to give nothing than a piece of crap gift. I can remember receiving a tee shirt with a really nice logo of the gifting company on it. It was a size XL and when washed, it became a child's medium. It was worse than worthless. I have never forgotten this and have always thought of this particular company as "cheap." I would rather spend a little more and have a customer say, "Hey, *nice shirt!*" At the very least, think about how something like this affects your image.

I almost forgot, personally sign your cards. I mean the gift cards, greeting cards, Christmas cards, anything that you send, and if it just has your name or company name *imprinted* on it, it needs to be signed in hand. I once had this real macho buyer flip a birthday card he received across to his desk at me. "These people don't even have the good manners to sign the card." He thought that the card might as well have said "Yada yada yada." I never forgot it and always pass this on when I can.

Lesson learned: What you do is a reflection on you. Good manners are remembered.

Chapter Fourteen:

Maraschino Drink Story

I put this story in here because it is important to realize that some customers are so unique that they might not fit in with your competition's theory of what they tolerate in a customer. This could mean that a lucrative account with a real jerk in purchasing could be *your* lucrative account, and it may turn out that the guy just takes getting used to.

We went out to an upscale restaurant in downtown Charleston. I had brought my girlfriend since the buyer had brought his wife. It was the first time I had met the wife. She was the exact opposite of her husband. She was well dressed, polite, and reserved. Everything was going fine until the waiter came and asked if we would like to order drinks. At this time, I got an inkling that the wife was not going to get to order anything without first being interrogated about her choice by the husband. She said that she would like a standard drink of some kind except that it was not going to be standard. Instead of one ingredient, she wanted to substitute some exact amount of juice from the Maraschino Cherry jar that is usually stocked in all bars. At first look, this did not seem like a problem. I was soon to find out that a storm was brewing.

The waiter soon returned with our drinks, and all was well until the wife sampled hers. She closed one eye, stuck out her tongue, and her head began to vibrate in all directions at once. She gagged several times while the girlfriend and I covered our glasses. The husband immediately grabbed the glass and took his own sip. "Aaaakkk." He did a move which was so much like the wife it appeared they had rehearsed. It was like they had been tasered. He looked in the glass like he was expecting to see eye of newt. The poor waiter asked if anything was wrong. The husband said that there was a tad too much Maraschino Cherry juice. He then gave the young waiter precise instructions to tell the bartender exactly how to make the drink properly. I can only imagine the conversation in the bar. I only know that the second drink elicited the exact same response from husband and wife. At this point, my girlfriend and I had begun to view the episode as entertainment. We were anxiously awaiting their third drink as we had now ordered another round for ourselves.

When the third drink arrived, it was also unacceptable, but, because of time considerations, they were forced to give in and drink it anyway. I was looking forward to the fourth to see if something else could possibly happen.

What I later realized was that this guy was going to be in charge of somebody everywhere he went, first his wife, then the bartender. He was like Hitler without the armband. He didn't have time to get to me.

The funny thing is that he had a great time and evidently really liked me. I called that drink cement because it was the foundation we built on. I took him out many more times and on at least three more occasions in different establishments, the cherry juice drink order played out almost exactly the same. I think that each bartender may have a sketch of him behind the bar for reference.

I often thought that the third or fourth drink that was accepted and drank may have had saliva as the secret ingredient.

Lesson learned: Don't confuse the worth of a customer with his behavior. Being a good customer has its privileges.

Chapter Fifteen:

Greatest Mistakes

I was having supper with a woman who was one of my larger customers that I had known for years. We always got along great, and she sometimes shared problems and events that occurred in her life and job. This particular night, she had told me about a problem, so I suggested a way to handle it. No big deal right? Well, I learned a valuable lesson that evening.

When I looked at her again, she was looking at me like I stepped in dog crap and had just scraped it off on the edge of her plate. I asked if something was wrong and she said, "Nope." "Are you sure? " I said, "You look upset." "Nope." I have been married. I know what "Nope" means. It means the opposite of nope. One minute I am sitting there happier than a dingo in a nursery, and the next minute my customer is angry, and I am clueless. I asked if it was something I had done and got a nod. I apologized and asked what it was so I would not do it again. Of course, she refused to tell me. Now it has gone from me taking a customer out to dinner to a "date" atmosphere. To make a long story short, she finally told me that when I had suggested a solution to her problem, I was telling her how to do her job. I read *Men are from Mars and Women Are from Venus* and this is covered in the book, and I immediately "got it."

Lesson learned: If you deal with women in either your business life or personal life, read the book. I mean it; read the book. It comes recorded so you can get it at the library and listen to it in the car, too.

Chapter Sixteen:

Checking Up On the Salesman

If you are a sales manager, you might be interested in my views on managing. I have viewed it from the purchasing side as well as the selling side. I've seen good and bad.

First, let me say that if the salesman is good, it will be obvious in his sales records. Even excellent salesmen will sometimes meet purchasing people that they are not compatible with and be unable to sell to these individuals. It is inevitable. Let it go. Chalk it up to human nature or whatever. If you "investigate" this excellent salesman and his customers take offense to your tactics, you could lose the confidence of the customer, and when the customer tells the salesman why, you could lose this valuable employee. Be smart when you check up on someone who does not need to be checked up on.

Example: When I was in purchasing, I had an excellent steel salesman calling on me. He knew his stuff, was a nice guy and I liked him. One day two guys from the home office came in to see me unannounced. They acted like detectives, asking me questions about how the salesman did his job. The manner in which it was done really irritated me. I relayed this to the salesman, and he said that several other customers had already told him about it. Within a year, the salesman found employment with another steel company.

On the other hand, if the salesman is not doing well and is not making quota, then it would be a good thing to find out why. I had a salesman call on me one time that had left a bloody swath across the state by flying off the handle if anything happened that was unexpected, like a long wait in a lobby. He would rant, insult the company, and offend the receptionist. This is the mild stuff. I later found that he often did much worse. When the owners of his company visited a year later, they told me about the wreckage caused and that the guy was actually in a sanatorium and not expected to ever leave it. Maybe they should have checked up on him sooner. I am certain that his sales record was poor.

I once followed up on a salesman that had been writing up glowing call reports of how he was going to get business from certain accounts soon. I called one prospect and asked if there was anything my company could do better to go ahead and get started with them. I was told they had never seen a salesman from our company. Oops. I called two more and got the same answer. That was the end of that relationship and too bad because the guy had the talent to be a good salesman…just not the ethics.

The problem with mailing out a "how are we doing" survey to your customers is that you will miss the feedback from these non-customers that might tell you of a problem. It is worth thinking about and formulating a plan that works and does not offend your customer base. Making a list and making periodic joint calls with the salesman is always one option. You make the list.

Chapter Seventeen:

Toleration

First let me say that I was in purchasing in a past life and knew the power I had over salesmen. I had the complete discretion of who to buy from, how much, and when. I was in my mind, The God of Purchasing. Some purchasing people who have this power use it for good (like me) others, for evil. They denigrate all salespeople who come before them. They are hated by most all salespeople.

Given time, all salespeople will run into these jerks. After a first encounter with one of these guys, some salespeople don't wish to waste their time putting up with an abusive asshole and go on to greener pastures. I went on to greener pastures after my first encounter, too.

What I learned later was that if there is some way that you can get on the good side of this jackass, then you have an account that is almost an exclusive. My competitors were few and far between because they had better opportunities elsewhere. Let me say that the pernicious individual has to work hard for an account that is worthwhile dollar wise, and if it is, the rewards of having a large account that competitors are loath to call on is really nice.

My advice, based on success of great monetary gain, is that when you meet up with one of these assholes, find a way to get by their attitude, and you might just uncover that, given you are a good salesman, you can find a way to not only tolerate this person, but you can even find a part of him to accept. (See chapter 13)

Lesson learned: The bigger the purchasing jerk, the lesser the competition. The lesser the competition, the easier the sale.

Chapter Eighteen:

The Dave

I told this story about a friend of mine to my boss, and he thinks it is his favorite illustration of what not to do that I have related to him. I believe that he has used it and may have even given me credit for the illustration.

My friend, let's call him Dave, is a very intelligent guy and is really good with the technical stuff and fancies himself a problem-solver. This is a two edged sword as you will see. Dave was telling me this sales story and how he was screwed over by this buyer. It seems that Dave went in to see this new account on a problem. Dave latched right on to the situation and suggested a solution to engineering which they liked. After a few samples and testing, they bid the item. (Dave solves a problem and then has to be the low bidder?) Anyway, somehow, Dave was fortunate enough to be close on the bid to get the order for the business, and it was a _really_ big order. Sometimes things just happen to go right.

Well, not necessarily. Dave, in the Purchasing Agent's office with order (<u>big order</u>) in hand, says to the buyer, "You know, I could save you some money if you could take these in black…" I need to skip a line so that you can feel the silence and dread after

reading that line. If you are an experienced salesman, you probably already know that the Purchasing Agent held up on the order and yes, after checking with engineering…_went back out for bids in **black**!_ Of course, Dave lost the second bid and blamed it all on that no-account Purchasing Agent, the one who had already given him the order.

I call that "**Pulling A Dave.**" You may see something similar happen or hear about it from time to time. Hopefully, if it happens to you because you try and do the right thing, it will not cost you a big order. Maybe seeing this in print will remind you to get the hell out of there with the order and after some period of time after you are firmly entrenched as the supplier, you can offer the alternative of "black."

Lesson learned: Know when to shut up. Take the order and say,"Thanks."

Chapter Nineteen:

Sales Presentations

There will always be a few idiots in the audience when you put on a presentation for a group. There are usually one or two guys actually listening, so you have to be factual, and almost all of them can read. I have been to so many presentations and seminars that tried to put me to sleep that I could never estimate how many. I have a few rules that are in no particular order but bear perusing. I think most readers will agree with all of them, but sometimes it is nice to remember you are not alone.

If you are the presenter:

Rule 1:

Be on time. In fact, be early to set up. Believe this; being late will probably ruin anything you have to say and it will follow you forever.

Rule 2:

Never ever read your presentation word for word to the audience unless you are in a Book Guild reciting from some poetic stuff.

Rule 3:

Never give a hand out that you plan to read (see rule number 1) verbatim to the audience.

Rule 4:

Never give a hand out copy of your presentation until the presentation is over. Most will scan it ahead of you and try and get some sleep while you drone on. If yours is a presentation that may require extensive notes being taken, you could reconsider this rule, but I believe I would abbreviate the outline to eliminate some of the snoring.

Rule 5:

Never put your presentation in a slide show format and point out to everyone exactly what you just said. You don't have to *prove* that you just said something. It is especially annoying to the audience when you try to slow them down by displaying only one line at a time. Many will not be listening *or* reading because they are either highly intelligent and cannot tolerate the inefficiency or do not have an attention span long enough for you to finish reciting the item in print.

Rule 6:

Never have an unqualified poor public speaker on the stage because his department needs to be included to round things out. Especially in Accounting. If there is someone in attendance who actually understands the Director of Accounting's input, he should not have been invited to the presentation in the first place. These guys will put a black splotch on your presentation that will not only ruin it but live on long after the day is done.

Rule 7:

Never begin your presentation right after lunch; the snoring will drown you out.

Rule 8:

One on one presentations are almost always best presented during lunch or supper. The audience is thankful for the meal, and if they try and fall asleep, they will get food on their face.

Rule 9:

Samples and demonstrations are things that almost everyone loves, especially engineers. Include them any time that you can.

Rule 10:

At the beginning of any and all presentations, tell the audience to interrupt whenever they have a question or comment. If you do this, you will have lots more audience participation, *and* it will be relevant to the topic. If you get an interruption early in the presentation, it will break the ice so others will participate. Answering a question is nearly always a good thing. As you grow in experience, you may be able to pick out the bad seeds that will ask questions that they already know the answer to. This will eventually make you stronger.

Rule 11:

Remember that if you ask the audience questions that they don't know the answer to, it makes them look stupid. Tread carefully when you use this approach.

Rule 12:

Never make really loud noises like slamming down a book

during your presentation as it will startle the half of the audience that is sleeping.

Chapter Twenty:

Sales Venue

During my entire sales career, I probably ate lunch with my customers or had supper with them on more than 80% of my visits. I have this theory that lots of buyers will go out to lunch with you for a free meal but, if during that free meal, you ask the guy if you will be able to do some business with him and he says "Yes," he most likely will. He is in an uncomfortable spot if he says "No," and you are paying for his lunch. If you are a decent salesman, and he wants to say no, he will probably give you some excuse on why he cannot do business with you at this time (Like he is in a contract). That is OK by me; I just ask when the contract is up, can we do some business? Now where does he go?

Going back to square one, none of the above will get you anywhere if the buyer doesn't like you or you work for a mediocre company. Otherwise, you should not go out to lunch with a prospective customer and not use at least some of that time to secure your place in the food chain. I had to take a factory salesman out with me to a very good prospect one time years ago, and I remember it like it was yesterday. The guy spent a good many years in college because he fooled around and partied a lot. He had what he thought were funny anecdotes of drunken college escapades. We were having lunch with this buyer who I didn't know all that well. I was trying to tell her about my company, and this guy would interrupt every time he got the chance and tell yet another of his wild stories. The lad even would turn to me after he finished and say something like, "What was that you were saying?" I accomplished very little during that long trip and excellent opportunity. I have never forgotten the lesson learned.

I know that there are good salesmen who think that you should wait until after lunch to talk business. I happen to disagree, and I have the money to prove my point. I don't encourage business *all* through the meal, but get **something** accomplished if you can. I can't count how many times I have returned from lunch with a customer and when we hit the door to his office, either the phone rang or there was an urgent message, and he had to tell me he would have to go and would see me next trip.

At the very least, use the technique in Chapter Five so that when you encounter a bidding problem maybe you already handled it.

Note: When a customer says, "I was out with (another supplier), and we went to (place in town) and had a really good meal," you need to know what that means. If you don't, you need to find out. It's like one of those old adages, "If you have to ask, the answer probably won't help you."

Lesson learned: When you are having a good time or spending quality time with a client, make the most of it.

Chapter Twenty One:

Making the Most of a Good Situation

One time I was in my car on the way to see a customer when I received an urgent phone call from my boss. Our biggest customer had a rejection because of a failure of one of our gaskets. If there is anything good about this, it would be that it was not a problem with our function of cutting the gasket but more likely bad gasket *material*. This company put out thousands of product per day so that any problem like this is a massive one with huge cost implications and recalls or re-builds. All of this was running through my mind, when I realized that the company that made the material almost <u>never</u> makes a bad product. Then I jumped to the conclusion that *we* might be the enemy. Somehow we had used the wrong material! Then I thought that was even less likely than the manufacturer screwing up. Anyway, I called my office back to see how many gaskets we had shipped and when. Then the sun came out. We had not shipped that gasket for months. We even had a safety stock on our shelves for an emergency since this customer often ran out of parts. This was really good news. I knew from experience that they must have purchased this lot of gaskets from a competitor because they only had enough parts shipped to them to last a short time because of inventory costs. There was no way these gaskets were from us. Whew!

Now the good part. An engineer met me at the door, and we hurried back to the plant. On the way, he showed me the burned to a crisp gaskets that had failed. I immediately saw that they were the wrong material. They were not even close to the correct material that was specified on their prints. We met the head of Quality Control and a bunch of concerned people on the way, and I made sure that they all knew that this was a terrible thing, and I felt concerned that anything could possibly come out of our system of controls like this. I brought up their likely expenses and how we would get the correct material to them that same day to minimize their production shut down. When I saw all the burnt gaskets that they had laid out in the lab, I asked to see the shipping container. They still had several boxes that they had opened to look at. Not one of them had noticed that the gaskets came from my competitor. We had been their primary supplier for 30 years, and no one even had in inkling that these gaskets came from someone else. Of course, I fell silent. After they called the buyer to come down and see the mess he had put them in, I offered to save the day and have gaskets in their plant within the hour.

I know that there are other people who would not have handled this golden opportunity the same way that I did. I also know that it was lucky that we discovered all the facts beforehand. Maybe it is just me, but I would do it this way again in a New York minute. How often do you think that the buyer even thought about switching an inexpensive yet critical item like a gasket after all of the trouble and expense this cost?

The other big benefit of this story is that I told it over and over during meals instead of funny drunken college anecdotes.

Lesson learned: When the opportunity presents itself, don't miss out on the rewards. They may be worth more than you ever imagined.

Chapter Twenty Two:

Bad Mouthing the Competition

You never know who might be a brother-in-law of the competition, so I always thought the practice was dangerous ...unless they deserve it. In any case, I don't think it is in your best interest to *blatantly* badmouth a competitor. Like, if you say, "Are you getting many rejections from them?" Or, "Are they ever late on delivery?" Both of those questions could be construed as inflammatory, even so, they are legitimate. By the way, EVERYONE is late sometime. I just find it hard not to say *something* after a competitor has done something really terrible like underbidding the wrong material and they, after getting the order, saying they made a mistake as the *real* material is somewhat higher. Now the buyer has already spent money on a tool with this company, and bingo he is in like Flynn. Another thing, who is this Flynn guy, and how does he get in?

After you get to know a customer for a good length of time, of course all of this flies out the window. I have had buyers tell me really bad things that they experienced with a competitor, so at that juncture I think it is OK for me to tell a story that I heard. Like this one: (I will leave out the competitor's name).

I was out at the Power Company looking at some really expensive parts that they were buying from a competitor I had heard bad things about in the past. It just so happens that I was familiar with the material that was called out for these parts, and it was in fact manufactured *especially* for this application. It was a premium type material because it was a critical application. I took one look and knew that the material was not the right stuff. I told the foreman this, and he got all upset. This was great! Sort of like getting a lap dance from Selma Hayek only in the parts room of a warehouse. I drove uptown to the Purchasing Department and related what I had found out there and suggested that they could call the manufacture of the real material to confirm my opinion, and they did. I got an order for the parts and thought that was the end of it. Nope. It got worse.

The best part for me was that when I went back to see the Purchasing Agent, he told me that he had called the other supplier and told him to come and pick up his bad parts that were not to spec. Well, this competitor called Engineering and set up a meeting to get his material approved behind the PA's back. Whoa! Bad move. If there was a black list, this company was on it. In this case I was able to say that I heard a worse story that happened with this same company in a nuclear facility.

Still, all in all, I think pushing your own company and letting the competition fend for itself usually is the best course. A bad competitor is like a new tie. Sooner or later it will be spotted.

Lesson learned: Pay attention to mistakes of the competition. You might benefit from them.

Chapter Twenty Three:

Dining With Clients

It is incredible how many lessons I have learned over the years. I have tried to profit by each of them. I would have argued that this is no big deal if handled correctly and that *could* be the case. I think that if you are wrong, it could cost you a lot of business.

Never make a scene in a restaurant while dining with a client. NEVER. You might think that this is a no-brainer, but believe me, if your client has a problem with the service or his food, you might feel obligated to step in and handle the situation because you are the host. This might end up with you as the "bad guy," and it could ruin the whole evening. I have been all around this situation for over 30 years and, as I look back, I know I was just plain lucky to escape with my reputation unscathed several times.

It is a real shame to be out at a nice restaurant with a good customer or worse, *prospective* customer and his wife, and, in the end after all the trouble and expense, all that will be remembered is how you embarrassed them by arguing or complaining. Ouch!

I also think it is a mistake to relate stories of how you had trouble in the past with some waiter or restaurant. If you get going and tell several stories about these incidents that you think are good conversation, it may start to look like *you* are the problem. I myself have thought this when other people have told me a series of food stories. The other guy is *always* the bad guy. You don't need that risk with a client.

One story that I am especially proud to relate happened rather late in my career. I say that because I had learned a few things by that time. I was out in a supposedly really fine restaurant. If you cannot tell by the décor if the restaurant is "fine," you can just look at the prices on the menu. Anyway, I was out with a lady client and expected a leisure evening without much pressure because I already did a good amount of business with her. Well, things went bad from the start. We were seated almost immediately because the place was practically empty except unbeknownst to us, there was a big party in a back room. It took about 20 minutes to get a waitress. I asked the young lady who finally came out of the back somewhere if they were shorthanded tonight. She said no and that she would bring the drinks we ordered right out. Right out was another 20 minutes. We had been discussing the delay and wondered whether our waitress had been abducted by aliens on the way to the kitchen when she finally appeared. She apologized about the delay, and I casually asked what caused it. Really, it was *feigned* casual but, nevertheless, I was nice about it and appeared to be what I like to call James-Bond-like suave. Stupid us, we let the waitress go without ordering food. When the waitress finally reappeared, our glasses had long dried up, and she looked somewhat older. People that have been marooned were not as thirsty as we were. We ordered another round of drinks to be brought "right out" as well as the food to be served soon after. Calm and cool, I did elicit a promise for the waitress to come right back with the drinks. Nope.

Well, to make a long story short, things got worse and by the time we got our food, we were no longer hungry. My steak was so cold on the inside I thought of asking for an ice pick instead of a knife but restrained myself. The owner came over when we were leaving and told us that the ruined evening and meal was not her fault. They had this big party in the back and had to give them preference. Believe it or not, that did not make it any better.

The reason I am writing about this is because of the lesson I learned. For years after this night, the customer would bring it up in front of others about how I handled the situation. She thought that my NOT getting upset was something memorable. Of course my close non-business friends don't believe a word of it. It is true nonetheless.

Lesson learned: Anyone can get pissed off at bad service, but if you handle it like a gentleman, someone may actually think you are a gentleman. And... it counts!

Chapter Twenty Four:

Alcohol

Since I advocate socialization with customers, which includes having a few drinks with them when the opportunity presents itself, I thought I should mention the following story.

Many years ago when I was a purchasing agent, I often went out with suppliers. One time when I showed up at his motel to pick up this salesman, he came out to the car drunk. He was staggering and slurring his words. I would have rather had a case of the clap than go out to eat with this guy. Prior to this, he had always been a regular guy, and I liked him but now things had changed. I tried to cancel out and go back home, but he begged me to stay. He said he would be OK in a few minutes. On the ride to the restaurant, he blubbered himself halfway semi-sober, and during the meal, he actually became partly intelligible. It was too late. I lost all respect for the man because I guess in the back of my mind, he had no respect for me, his company, or my company.

I have never forgotten this night, and whenever I have been in a situation to maybe have a drink or two over the line, I have stopped cold. I believe that almost anyone that is put in a situation like the story above will react similarly at least subconsciously if not right up front. It will haunt you forever if you lose a big account because of it, especially since you read this chapter. I know that if the client is inebriated (too), you might get away with over-imbibing, but don't bet your career on it.

I can remember one time I was in Shreveport and was out with a buyer who was really a big drinker. He could hold quite a few drinks, and I think I can too, but, I was not going to get into a contest with him. After three drinks, I met the waitress at the bar and told her that no matter what I order from then on, she was to bring me a diet coke. The buyer had several more, and had I tried to keep up, I would have needed a walker to get to the bathroom. Everything went well that evening and although I always thought my diet coke ploy was cool, I never had to use it again.

I realize that most good salesmen already know all of this alcohol stuff, but it never hurts to jog a memory lest you are tempted.

Lesson learned: It's better to actually be in control than think you are in control.

Chapter Twenty Five:

Perception

If you want to look it up, there seems to be many "originators" of the quotation: "**Perception is reality**." It is not a difficult premise to grasp. If you think something is a fact, even if it isn't, to you it is because you perceive it to be. You can set up certain circumstances where you can probably prove the opposite but, for me, concerning the person you are selling to, it matters what that person thinks the facts are…even and maybe *especially* if he is wrong.

In my mind, the most likely times that this will occur is when someone perceives behavior as rude, condescending, or disrespectful. They my think you are a smart-aleck when you thought you were being amusing. Believe this: If they **think** you are out of line with something, you have done or said, you **are.**

I can't tell you how many times an upset buyer has said to me,

"You know what this guy *said?*" Taking the other guy's side in my mind, I knew that was not what the guy meant to portray. The buyer just took it wrong. It is much worse in a letter or e-mail. What is meant as funny sarcasm can go horribly wrong.

At my company, often when we had an important letter go out to a customer, if I wrote it, I would have my boss read it to see if I said anything that could be misconstrued, and he would have me read some of his for the same reason. More often than not, each of us would suggest re-wording some part of the letter just in case it could be taken the wrong way. Cheap insurance.

Many times my boss and I would have a disagreement about how to handle a situation with a customer and even though my boss would be totally correct in his thinking, I would point out that the customer would not see it that way. Even if we were right, we would ultimately attempt to handle the point at issue with the customer's position in mind.

Lesson learned: If something can be taken the wrong way, it probably will be.

Chapter Twenty Six:

Other Stuff

Buyers are like spouses. They hold on to things you say....

forever. I can remember this one buyer who I sold to for 25 years.

When I first called on him, he told me that one of my competitors

was late on a delivery and that he had to call and expedite several

times. That morning, they had told him that every time he called,

they had to phone their supplier and that they were going to have

to start billing him for their calls to their supplier. No kidding.

They actually said that. He told me that story a dozen times over

the years. Ouch. I have heard tales from other salespeople of

how they had called on the wrong guy. One had taken a buyer to

lunch for years, and the guy never revealed that he was not the

buyer of his product. One of our best customers came up with this

great idea of splitting cost improvements. Their revolutionary

idea was that for any cost savings, we could come up with by implementing new manufacturing concepts instead of telling them about it and they just thanking us; they would split the cost savings with us for a whole year. The buyer who was asked to travel to all their suppliers and relay this concept had chosen us as his first stop. After he had made his presentation, I asked, "So the deal is we save you, say, $1000 dollars on a cost reduction idea, and we split the $1000 so that we get $500 for the first year and you get $500 for the first year, and then you get $1000 dollars for the next 20 years or so?" (They seldom changed a design). There was a long pause. He said it doesn't sound as good put that way, does it?

We have a Manufacturing Engineer (and most all of them think this way) who has espoused the theory that it is the (quality) manufacturing that "gets the customers." Of course, he is wrong. It is the quality manufacturing that helps KEEP the customers. **I** got the customers. If that sounds like boasting, it is. If you are a good salesman, everybody usually knows it.

Lesson Learned: Know your audience. Look at things through their eyes before you pitch.

Summary

This book was never meant to be a how-to book. It is meant to be a book to jog the memory or subconscious of otherwise self-sufficient salesmen. If you are no good at selling, you probably will never make an excellent salesman no matter how much you read. If on the other hand, some of my experience will cause you to say to yourself, "You know that's a good idea," or "I should do more of that," then I have done my job.

I had several salespeople that I respect read the draft for this book before it was sent to a publisher and every one of them said that if anyone just gets even *one* of my points or techniques, it will be well worth the price of the book. I of course, agree.

I like to make lists. It makes things easier for me. The list I would make for this book is on the next page. If you are one of those people who march to a different drummer then maybe you should at least consider these points:

To be <u>really</u> successful in sales:

1. People must like you.

> Few people say, *"Here comes that obnoxious salesman again; let's get him up a big order."*

2. You need to work for a good company with a good product.

> Few people say, *" I really like that guy, but his company is worthless. Let's get him up a big order."*

3. You need to socialize with your customers.

4. Numbers one and two above will get you an order. Adding number three will get you a lifetime of orders.

www.ingramcontent.com/pod-product-compliance
Lightning Source LLC
Chambersburg PA
CBHW060405190526
45169CB00002B/765